Keep Them Thinking

- Level II -

A Handbook of Model Lessons

Robin Fogarty

SKYLIGHT
PUBLISHING, INC.
Palatine, Illinois

Other titles in this series:

Start Them Thinking

Catch Them Thinking

Teach Them Thinking

Keep Them Thinking: Level I (grades K-3)

Keep Them Thinking: Level III (grades 7-12)

Keep Them Thinking: Level II
Second Printing

Published by Skylight Publishing, 200 E. Wood Street, Suite 274, Palatine, Illinois, 60067
1-800-348-4474, in northern Illinois 1-708-991-6300, FAX 1-708-991-6420

Editing: Sharon Nowakowski
Type Composition: Donna Ramirez
Book Design: Bruce Leckie
Illustrations: Jim Arthur

ISBN 0-932935-05-2

Foreword

Our children are the messages we send to a time we will not see.
—Betty Seigle

The lessons in this series are designed with three premises in mind: The teacher is the architect of the intellect. The student is the capable apprentice. And, thinking is more basic than the basics—it frames all learning.

Premise 1

The teacher is the architect of the intellect.

A teacher affects eternity. He never knows where his influence ends.

—Henry Adams

As an architect of the intellect, a teacher leaves his mark on history. The classroom teacher is, above all else, a designer of learning, an expert craftsman who knows content, understands child development, and manages young people with finesse.

The excellent teacher skillfully crafts the lesson with a clear purpose. Just as form follows function for the traditional architect, the structure of the lesson is determined by the learning goal.

Aesthetically, lessons are designed to invite the learner in. When the design is exquisite, the invitation becomes irresistible to the learner. He enters the learning situation excited and with a level of expectancy that sets the scene for motivated learning.

Premise 2

The student is the capable apprentice.

'Come to the edge,' he said. They said, 'We are afraid.'
'Come to the edge,' he said. They came.
He pushed them . . . and they flew.

—Apollinaire

Believing that the student is capable of becoming the master of his own learning is sometimes difficult for the architect mentor. But through carefully crafted instruction, exemplary, consistent modeling, and deliberate practice, the apprentice learns. Only then, by relinquishing the honored role of master architect, is the student free to advance on his own.

To believe one is capable is to let go. It is to trust and to watch as the learner takes over—and goes beyond—for he is the capable apprentice.

Premise 3

Thinking is more basic than the basics—it frames all learning.

Intelligent behavior is knowing what to do when you don't know what to do.

—Arthur Costa

Thinking is the foundation for all learning. To say we're going to teach thinking in our classroom does not imply that we don't already do just that. Of course we teach thinking, but now by focusing on cognitive behavior, thinking becomes the blueprint from which we design and structure learning.

The blueprint of thinking becomes the reference that guides our instructional decisions. And, as the architect of the intellect, we concern ourselves as much with the process as with the final product. We select materials with care and deliberation. We direct activities with skill and closely monitor the progress. Finally, with a feeling of pride and accomplishment, we stand back and view the masterpiece—in this case a cadre of young people—thinking and learning in self-directed ways.

Robin Fogarty

Contents

Contents

Introduction

Keep Them Thinking: Level II presents thinking lessons and activities designed especially with the middle grades in mind. Intermediate and junior high school students are equipped with a cadre of basic skills in reading, writing, and speaking. By integrating a deliberate thinking component into the content lessons, students are able to develop and refine "patterns for thinking." These explicitly taught thinking skills are the prerequisites for effective problem-solving, decision making and creative ideation. These are tools for life.

Three fully developed thinking skill lessons covering a spectrum of mental processes are detailed for immediate classroom use:

Creative Thinking

A creative thinking skill, **brainstorming**, is developed through the acronym SCAMPER—Substitute, Combine, Adopt, Modify, Put to other use, Eliminate, Reverse. The strategies introduced in this brainstorming technique lead students toward a deliberate visualization approach to generating and producing ideas.

Critical Thinking

A critical thinking skill, **analyzing for bias**, causes youngsters to think analytically and evaluatively. This skill presents bias clues that students can search for as they become more critical thinkers. The clues developed include: exaggeration, overgeneralization, imbalance, opinion stated as fact, and charged words.

Problem Solving

In the final section, an adaptation of the Parnes and Noller *Creative Problem Solving* model is presented. It encompasses both creative, generative thinking, and critical, evaluative mental processing. The complete CPS model is elaborated.

Explicit Lessons

Each of the three skills, brainstorming, analyzing for bias, and problem solving are developed around a similar format. Each skill is explicitly taught in an introductory lesson with the objective clearly stated. Several short practice lessons are outlined to ensure internalization of the skill, and finally, several transfer lessons delineate the ease of bridging thinking skills into content areas and life situations.

The elaborated lesson design provides extensive plans for each of the three skills. The purpose of this elaboration is to provide models or templates for the teacher to adapt in designing explicit thinking skill lessons, practice exercises, and transfer lessons.

The **MODEL LESSONS** include:

Lesson Objective The skill for the lesson explicitly stated.

Key Vocabulary Vocabulary that may require clarification, explanation, and/or emphasis before, during and after the lesson.

Looking Back A brief statement to stir prior knowledge and to help relate the new information to previous experiences.

Getting Ready Background information, rationale, and premises that undergird the lesson.

At-A-Glance A synopsis of the lesson or the lesson in a nutshell.

Materials A quick reference list of all the materials you will need for the model lesson.

Focus Activity A short, anticipatory activity suggested to set the stage for the introduction of the new skill.

Activity Objective A concise statement of the purpose of the main activity.

Activity The interactive part of the classroom lesson, including the instructional input and the student participation.

Metacognitive Processing Reflective questions, activities, and discussion ideas about the lesson and the new skill.

Practice

To ensure students' internalization of the skill, short practices are outlined after the model lesson. The **Short Practices** offer suggestions for using the skills in your lessons and provide examples of exercises for relating that skill to familiar situations in students' everyday lives.

Transfer

Specifically tailored to activities in a variety of subject areas, the **Transfer Lessons** delineate the ease of bridging thinking skills across the curriculum. These shortened versions of the model lessons include: **Focus Activity, Objective, Activity, Structured Discussion, Metacognitive Processing,** and **Follow-up** (lesson extensions and enrichment ideas for both in and out of the classroom).

Evaluation

As a final step in ensuring student transfer and comprehension of the thinking skills presented, each chapter concludes with an **Evaluation of Skills**. You may use this section to further process the activities with your students or to measure, gauge or evaluate your students' development and understanding of the lessons.

Ongoing Transfer

The lessons presented provide a solid beginning to designing lessons for the teaching of critical and creative thinking in the classroom. These lessons should be viewed as generic patterns upon which to model personally relevant lesson plans as teaching thinking becomes an integral part of all that we do in our interactions with students.

Creative Thinking Level II

Brainstorming

Thinking Skill: *Brainstorming*

Whatever one man is capable of conceiving, other men will be able to achieve.

—Jules Verne

Model Lesson:

Lesson Objective   To identify a deliberate process for brainstorming ideas.

Key Vocabulary   SCAMPER, hitchhike, piggyback, defer, DOVE, fluency, flexibility, elaboration, originality.

Looking Back   Previous experiences in the classroom have afforded students opportunities to practice generating ideas, making lists and thinking imaginatively. Students have visualized themselves as heroes; they've fantasized about living in another era; they've written long lists of synonyms and antonyms. They can, with some measure of success, think fluently and imaginatively.

Getting Ready   The need for creative thinking is clear as you reflect on a quote from Alex Osborn's book *Applied Imagination*: "Everything in the world remains to be done or done over. The greatest picture hasn't been painted. The ideal labor contract is yet unwritten. A windproof match, an airtight bottle cap, a lifetime lead pencil have not yet been conceived. The best way to train salesmen, an easy way to keep slim, a better way to pin diapers—all of these problems are unsolved. Not one product has ever been manufactured, distributed, advertised or sold as efficiently as it should be or someday must be. . . ."

A critical step in the creative thinking process is the skill of brainstorming, the kind that generates fluent lists of possibilities.

Brainstorming is not a difficult skill, but the process can be greatly enhanced by an awareness of the elements inherent in creative thinking, by applying an identified technique systematically to the generative process, and by following some basic guidelines as you facilitate the process. As a teacher of creative thinking, you can instruct students how to use this method to increase the fluency, flexibility, elaboration, and originality of their ideas.

To facilitate brainstorming, a "systematic search" provides a comprehensive approach. Some concrete examples will clarify. A man wanted a bookmark that would stay in place. He happened to be an employee of 3M, the company that manufactures a wide variety of adhesive materials. His idea was to develop an adhesive for the bookmark that would stick just enough to mark the pages in his hymn book at church, but unsticky enough to allow for easy removal with no damage to the page. He basically minified the stickiness factor of adhesive tape when he conceived the subsequently developed Post-It Note! In addition, since these sticky fellows have hit the market place, an avalanche of uses have appeared, illustrating the ingenuity and fluent thinking of the consumer.

The creator of the Big Clip did just the opposite. He *magnified* the standard paper clip, *substituted* plastic for metal and *modified* it by using color. People in a tragic, real-life episode survived through their creative ingenuity. By putting a safety pin to another use, they made a fishhook that helped them survive their 112-day ordeal at sea in a rubber raft.

To help students generate ideas, keep the following in mind:

1. **Elements of Creativity**

   Fluency - quantity
   Flexibility - shifts
   Elaboration - detail
   Originality - uniqueness

2. **SCAMPER Techniques***
   Substitute
   Combine
   Adapt
   Modify, magnify or minify
   Put to other uses
   Eliminate or elaborate
   Reverse, rearrange

3. **Rules for Brainstorming— DOVE**

   Defer judgment
   Opt for original and off-beat
   Vast numbers are important
   Expand on ideas by hitch-hiking

* Printed with permission, *Scamper,* D.O.K. Publishers, Buffalo, NY 14224

At-A-Glance You will initiate the development of this skill with a focus activity that requires students to practice their fluency in generating a list of ideas, shift their focus to demonstrate flexibility in adding to the original list and then to elaborate on the ideas presented. Next, you will introduce the key vocabulary and demonstrate by example the SCAMPER[1] technique. You will structure small-group, forced-response tasks to help all students generate ideas. Finally, you will direct transfer activities in which students apply the skill to a variety of subject areas and real-life situations.

[1]Robert Eberle's acronym for Osborn's checklist in *Applied Imagination*.

Focus Activity

1. Prepare the class for a random brainstorming activity by outlining the DOVE guidelines. Ask students to elaborate on the meaning of each letter and to theorize why each guideline is important. Post the DOVE guidelines for all to see.

2. Experiment with brainstorming. Present this hobbit-hole quote from J.R.R. Tolkien's *The Hobbit*:

   In a hole in the ground, there lived a hobbit. Not a nasty, dirty, wet hole, filled with ends of worms and an oozy smell, nor yet a dry, bare, sandy hole with nothing in it to sit down on or to eat; it was a hobbit-hole, and that means comfort.

   Ask students to respond spontaneously to the lead-in:

   My favorite place to create, my hobbit-hole, is _____.

   As you "whip" around the class, have each student respond in turn or say, "I pass," which is always an option. Record the statements as they are voiced. Then, do the next whip:

   One thing I need in my hobbit-hole is _____.

   Encourage students to follow the DOVE guidelines, especially when divergent ideas are listed in the second whip.

3. Now, introduce SCAMPER on an overhead. Explain that this is a deliberate approach to brainstorming that provides a comprehensive and visual search for alternative ideas.

Materials Needed

- [ ] Posters of DOVE, SCAMPER and SCAMER Prompters
- [ ] Hobbit-hole Example on transparency
- [ ] SCAMPER transparency, overhead projector, extension cord and screen
- [ ] Handouts of SCAMPER prompters
- [ ] Elements of Creativity poster
- [ ] Newsprint, markers and tape for groups
- [ ] Thinking log

SUBSTITUTE:

Who else instead? What else instead? Other ingredient? Other material? Other process? Other power? Other place? Other approach? Other tone of voice?

COMBINE:

How about a blend, an assortment, an ensemble? Combine units? Combine purposes? Combine appeals? Combine ideas?

ADAPT:

What else is like this? What other idea does this suggest? Does something in the past offer a parallel? What could I copy? Whom could I emulate?

MODIFY:

New twist? Change meaning, color, motion, sound, order, form, shape?

   MAGNIFY:

What to add? More time? Greater frequency? Stronger? Higher? Longer? Thicker? Extra Value? Plus ingredient? Duplicate? Multiply? Exaggerate?

   MINIFY:

Smaller? Condensed? Miniature? Lower? Shorter? Lighter? Split up? Understate?

PUT TO OTHER USES:

New ways to use as is? Other uses if modified?

ELIMINATE:

Omit? What to subtract?

REVERSE:

How about opposites? Turn it backward? Turn it upside down? Reverse roles? Change shoes? Turn tables? Turn other cheek?

   REARRANGE:

Interchange components? Other pattern? Other layout? Other sequence? Transpose cause and effect? Change pace? Change schedule?

Printed with permission, *Scamper*, D.O.K. Publishers, Buffalo, NY 14224

SCAMPER Brainstorming Prompters

Give examples for each letter as you explain the technique. For example:

> *Substitute:* Using staples to repair loose hem
> *Combine:* Wearing two and three earrings in one ear
> *Adapt:* Decorator phones
> *Modify:* Digital clocks
>   *Magnify:* The Concord airplane
>   *Minify:* The inflatable spare tire
> *Put to other uses:* Playpen becomes "pet pen"
> *Eliminate:* Windsurfer (eliminated rudder and tiller)
> *Reverse:* Finding destination on map; working backward
>   *Rearrange:* Piece of music

Ask students to generate additional ideas for each letter. Record these on the board or on a transparency. Remind students to follow the DOVE guidelines.

Activity Objective To practice the SCAMPER technique by identifying climate and conditions that are conducive to creative thinking.

Activity Post the *Lesson Objective* and highlight the word *brainstorming* by identifying the DOVE guidelines and the elements of creativity. Also post the DOVE, Elements of Creativity and SCAMPER posters. Next, provide handouts of the SCAMPER prompters. Review the examples of the technique that were presented earlier and elicit new ones from the students. Clarify any part of the technique that seems confusing to students. Conclude with a re-emphasis of the goal statement. Now, you and your students are ready to SCAMPER a hobbit-hole.

1. Using one of the cooperative group structuring methods, divide students into groups of three. The student with the earliest birth date in the year will set up the newsprint and record. The student with the next birth date will lead. The student with the latest birth date will keep time and manage the materials.

   a. **Recorder:** Records group answers on chart

   b. **Leader:** Manages in-turn responses, keeps answers on task and monitors DOVE

   c. **Materials Manager:** Picks up materials, keeps clean sheets taped to wall, supplies new tape and markers as needed and keeps a check on the time

   d. **Timekeeper:** Signals time

2. Demonstrate with a finished newsprint model that you have prepared as you give the task instructions.
   a. "Each group will conclude this task with lists that have a format similar to this example. Make your lists readable."

Hobbit-hole Example

Hobbit-holes 1	Hobbit-holes 2	Hobbit-holes 3
Substitute 1. Stereo for T.V.	**Modify** 1.	**Put to Other Uses** 1.
Combine 1. Headphone & Stereo	**Magnify** 1.	**Eliminate** 1.
	2.	2.
Adapt 1. TV tray for desk	**Minify** 1.	**Reverse** 1.
		Rearrange 1.

b. "We are going to use the SCAMPER technique to brainstorm ideas for creating the *ideal hobbit-hole*. Using the lists of places and things generated in the *Focus Activity*, SCAMPER a hobbit-hole. What are the possibilities? Imagine the ideal creative-thinking spot or environment as your group works through the deliberate 'SCAMPER search' for alternatives.

c. "When your turn comes, you may use any letter of SCAMPER to present your idea or you may say, 'I pass.' Do not take a lot of time to explain your idea now. Your trio will have 15 minutes to SCAMPER a hobbit-hole. Generate as many ideas as you can in that time. In brainstorming, the best ideas often come when the quantity of ideas increases."

3. At the end of 15 minutes signal students to complete the last idea and to focus on you for the next instruction.

4. "Look at your lists. Through discussion and voting, put an asterisk (*) next to any items on the list that all three of you agree should be included in the ideal hobbit-hole. Next, using all the items with an asterisk, and including others you personally find appealing, begin to design your ideal hobbit-hole. The design may be described verbally or sketched graphically. The ideal hobbit-hole designs are due _____. (You may want to announce that they'll share the designs through presentations that day.) You may use whatever time remains following your discussions and voting to begin your individual designs. At _____, we'll reconvene as one group."

5. Circulate among the groups. Look at the items. Listen for on-task discussion and encourage agreement. As groups complete the voting, facilitate the designing phase.

6. End the small-group sessions with a class discussion. Facilitate this by assembling students in a circle. When asking questions, remember to ask the question, wait for students to think, and then seek multiple responses. Assign a student to record questions.

   a. "In your own words, explain what brainstorming is." Ask clarifying questions after you select the first student. Repeat the question and let several other students answer in turn.

   b. "In your own words, explain the SCAMPER technique." Again, ask clarifying questions and accept several responses in turn.

   c. "What have you learned about brainstorming from this activity?" Continue accepting and encouraging in-turn responses until all aspects are covered. Everyone must respond in this segment. When you are satisfied with the list, ask the students to signal their level of understanding—100% (thumbs up); less than 99% (thumbs sideways); major confusion (thumbs down). For the latter two, have students identify the difficulty, clarify the questions, and ask other students who signaled thumbs up to respond. At a minimum, each student should be able to (1) define brainstorming, (2) define SCAMPER, and (3) give examples for each letter. When all students signal 100% understanding, do the concluding activity, *Metacognitive Processing*.

Metacognitive Processing

Instruct students to complete one of the following lead-ins in their Thinking Logs (use Overhead).

Brainstorming helps . . . .

I would like to SCAMPER . . . .

I wonder how. . . .

The part of SCAMPER that was the hardest for me was . . . .

SCAMPER is like _____ because . . . .

Thinking Logs

Writing crystallizes thought. With Thinking Logs you give your students the opportunity to:

- capture fleeting thoughts
- explore for understanding
- analyze for clarity
- synthesize into personal meaning
- make critical connections between new data and past experiences

Use Thinking Logs with your students to guide the "inking of their thinking" as they think to learn and learn to think.

Allow students three to five minutes to write. As you see the majority of them completing the log task, encourage the others to finish.

OPTIONAL   Ask for volunteers or whip around the class for responses to the lead-in:

Today, what I did well as a creative thinker was . . . .

As always, students have the option to say, "I pass." Accept all responses or give feedback to reinforce students' active participation and productive thinking.

Short Practices:

Focused practice is necessary reinforcement for each student to become familiar with this brainstorming method. In the process of having fun with the *deliberate search* of the SCAMPER technique, students automatically begin to use the variables when they need to generate ideas. As brainstorming is an integral part of all problem solving, the time devoted to the practice of this crucial skill is time well spent.

Additional short practices that follow the models used here may be necessary. So that all students become skilled at using SCAMPER in their own thinking, it is important that after each practice the class focuses on the SCAMPER variables and makes direct connections to personal instances of using the metacognitive brainstorming processes.

■ Using the media, students can become "SCAMPER Scouts." Have students use newspapers, magazines, radio and TV ads, to "scout out" the SCAMPER variables that make a product new and unique. Create a contest by forming teams within the class. As the "scouting" activities proceed, display the "evidence" of the SCAMPER innovations on a bulletin board. Have students use index cards to signify their scoutings from TV and radio. Some examples include:

1. Sweet 'n' Low - substituted (place under the S column)

2. Glitter nail polish - combined (place under the C column)

S	C	A	M	P	E	R
Sweet 'n' Low	*Glitter nail polish*					

Have students make a log entry with this lead-in:

What if I SCAMPER _____ . . . ?

(name a product)

■ Using this next activity, have students identify observable classroom behaviors and other traits of a creative thinker. Start by showing sketches of Leonard daVinci's visionary log entries, Edison's inventions, or Buckminister Fuller's innovations. This will help focus students on the creative thinking processes.

"In groups of three or four, use the attribute web to generate characteristics of a creative thinker by SCAMPERing. For example, what does he/she not do? (eliminate) How does he/she exaggerate? (magnify). Use the DOVE guidelines during this generative activity. Try to list as many traits and behaviors as you can. You will have five minutes."

Help any groups needing a spark or clarification as you move throughout the room. Reinforce specific behaviors and ideas that exemplify productive thinking. At the end of five minutes, get the group to focus on the next instruction.

"Using some or all of your SCAMPERed attributes, as a group, write a definition of a creative thinker. Once you've reached agreement, write your definition on large paper and tape it on the wall. You will have 10 minutes for this." Again, help groups as needed. After 10 minutes, have students finish. Discuss the definitions by asking one member of each group to present the group's thinking. Allow time for interaction.

If time allows, or the next day, have students regroup.

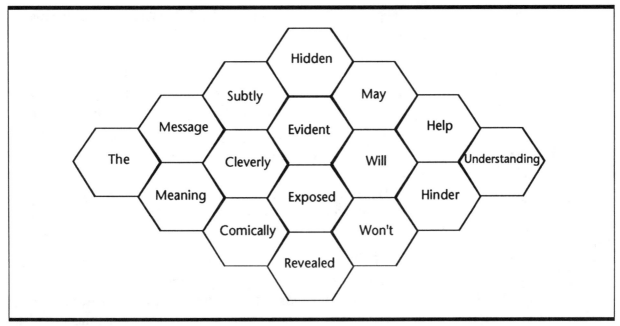

Sample Hex Message

"Using your definitions and ideas shared in our discussions, create a 'message of the hex' about a creative thinker. Use a hex structure like this (show sample hex message on board or overhead). As you manipulate words into the hex pattern, check that the message has meaning in any left-to-right reading." Explain and analyze the sample message.

Transfer Lesson: Math/ Story Problems

Focus Activity Ask students to turn to their neighbor or partner. Have one of the partners sing or recite the "Pledge of Allegiance," "The Star-Spangled Banner," the words to their favorite song, or the directions to get from school to their house. Next, let the other partner recite a song or directions.

Ask students how they learned to recite what they just did. What did they do to remember it (repeated over and over again, wrote it down, etc.)? Have them rank those strategies according to how much it helped them learn their songs or directions by heart. For example:

1. Repetition

2. Patterns (e.g. rhyme, melody)

3. Images (e.g. flash cards, sheet music, maps)

Objective To use the SCAMPER techniques to solve mathematical problems.

Activity After students have discussed their memorization strategies in the *Focus Activity*, begin this activity to help them develop their skill in brainstorming with the SCAMPER technique.

1. Begin by displaying the following question on an overhead transparency or the blackboard:

> What is the day after the day after tomorrow, if the day before the day before yesterday was Monday?

2. Divide the class into groups of four. The person with the longest last name in each group will lead the problem solving session. The person to the right will record calculations. The next person in rotation will observe, note and tell the strategies used. The last person will get the materials as needed.

3. Using the SCAMPER strategies, each group is required to work out a solution to the problem and record its work to reveal which strategies were used. The observer for the group lists the strategies used. The groups may use all or some of the SCAMPER variables. For example, they may minify by working the problem with smaller numbers to make it more manageable.

4. To facilitate students' problem solving, think about these possibilities listed below:

SCAMPER Examples

SCAMPER Strategy	Example
Substitute:	Use whole numbers for fractions; use an equation or formula; use smaller numbers.
Combine:	Sequence a series of steps to arrive at a final solution.
Adapt:	Use a graph, a chart, a picture, or a diagram.
Modify:	Round off, estimate or use a calculator.
Magnify:	Exaggerate to clarify or to check.
Minify:	Find smaller problems within the original problem.
Put to Other Uses:	Associate with similar problems you've solved before.
Eliminate:	What factors are relevant? What can you omit?
Reverse:	Start with the end result and work backward.
Rearrange:	Start with what you know, then go to an unknown; use manipulatives.

Printed with permission, *Scamper*, D.O.K. Publishers, Buffalo, NY 14224

5. "When you have agreed upon the answer, tape your two sheets on the wall, showing (1) your solution (recorder's sheet), and (2) your list of the SCAMPER strategies (observer's sheet). You will have 15 minutes to work on this."

#1 SOLUTION	#2 STRATEGIES

6. At the end of 15 minutes, have students finish the task and post their two sheets.

Structured Discussion

First, discuss the answers given. Second, in the process of justifying answers, have students use the *solution* worksheet to explain their thinking. After all the groups have justified their answers and have given explanations of their solutions, have the observers explain the strategies their groups used. Probe to find out how the groups chose to use those particular strategies. Next, compile a master list of the SCAMPER strategies used by the various groups and elicit student thinking about a) which strategies were most helpful or expedient, b) which strategies were not as appropriate for this problem, c) novel ways strategies were used that proved to be successful, and d) how they arrived at the best strategies.

Metacognitive Processing

Allow ample time to discuss the activity in depth. Remember to use wait time after posing questions to increase the interaction among students as they process the learning. Reinforce answers as you elicit the ideas. Encourage multiple answers as you point out that "there's more than one way to skin a cat." Remind students that choosing techniques depends on many variables:

- type of problem/level of difficulty
- prior knowledge
- learners' styles
- level of group collaboration
- flash of insight
- luck

Ask students to make a log entry at the end of the discussion. Try these lead-ins:

In this lesson, I learned that I . . . .

In this lesson, I was pleased that I . . . .

SCAMPERing seems . . . .

I was most impressed with . . . .

Follow-up Post this problem on the board or as a homework assignment:

> A man buys a horse for $50 and sells it for $60. He buys the horse back for $70 and then sells it again for $80. Did he earn or lose money, and how much? Or did he come out even?

SCAMPER is a search technique that promotes brainstorming. It provides alternatives and generates ideas on how situations can be viewed. SCAMPERing a problem of any sort focuses on discussions of a) solutions, b) how the answer is derived, c) what the students are thinking, d) how they are dealing with the information, and e) how they are processing the material. The answer is important as the catalyst for justifications, but *the process for getting there is the real learning focus.*

Transfer Lesson:
Language Arts/ Writing

Focus Activity Using the brainstorming strategies of SCAMPER, compile a list of famous people. Categorize the list of names—for example, artists and musicians, political leaders, scientists and inventors, authors and composers, athletes, and others. Have students select a famous figure. Students should gather as much information as they can on their person before the next class. Use the remainder of this class to research and gather information.

Objective To use the SCAMPER technique to write a creative and interesting biographical sketch.

Activity

1. Ask students to draw a circle on their paper. "Place the name

of your famous person inside the circle. On your own, brainstorm thoughts you have on your famous person using a mind map. Include any facts, images, sayings, or information you could include in a short, creative biographical sketch." Show the mind map on an overhead transparency.

2. **Mind Mapping** is an initial creative search that yields to a randomness of thoughts, yet stimulates "connections" to the center "trigger" circle. Tell students, "Just let your mind work. Jot down every connection or thought that pops into your head. There is no right way. Just let it happen. You'll have five minutes to see what happens."

3. After students have processed their personal brainstorms and clustered their thoughts about their famous figures, have them share their maps with a partner. Instruct students: "Find a partner. Share your mind maps. Tell how you made some of the connections. For example, when I thought of the human figure drawings, I remembered Leonardo daVinci also did scientific anatomical diagrams. After sharing your mind maps, use the

Mind Map Model

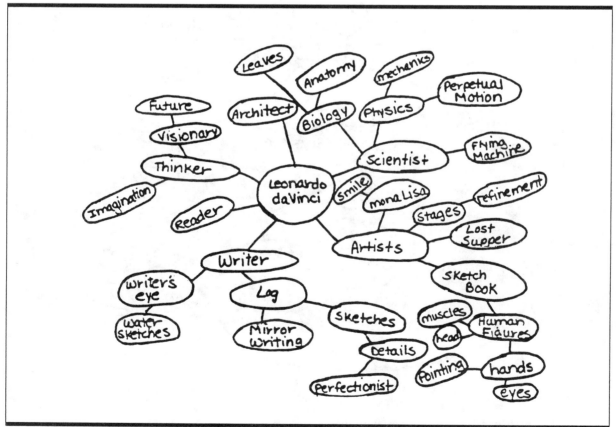

SCAMPER technique with your partner to embellish and refine your presentation ideas. (Be sure there is a poster of the SCAMPER technique visible in the classroom.) In this lesson, you will use the SCAMPER technique to clarify and focus your ideas. By using the SCAMPER technique you can choose to magnify one aspect of your cluster or to combine several ideas for writing an introduction about your genius. For example, I can minify my brainstorming by keying in on daVinci's log. Using the information from my SCAMPERing, I can introduce daVinci to you through his logs—not by telling you, 'He lived, he worked and he died.' You don't have to tell us everything about your genius. Give us bits and pieces in a creative and interesting way. Your presentation should entice other students into wanting to read more about your genius."

Have partners, SCAMPER their mind maps for a presentation by asking each other: How might you . . .

SCAMPERed Mind Map—Minified

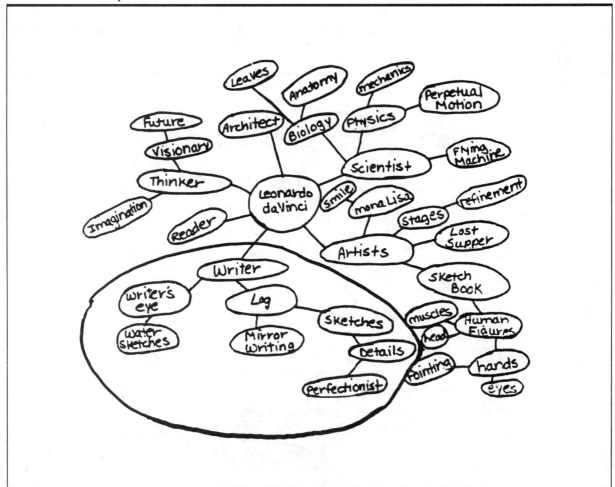

Substitute for a narrative? Use poetry? Try a dialogue?

Combine the most interesting aspects of his life?

Adapt some quotes or ideas she's famous for?

Modify the format? the focus? the misconceptions?

Minify by developing one small part?

Magnify a particular episode? Illuminate one aspect?

Put to other uses the information as a play? a skit? a TV interview? a speech?

Eliminate some information to get a better focus?

Reverse using flashback or retrospective?

Rearrange events or momentous achievements?

4. Generate other possible questions as you facilitate the partner work. Remember, by "wandering around," as illustrated by Peters and Austin in *A Passion for Excellence*, you are a barometer sensing the successes and challenges occurring in the groups. Be there when you're needed, but allow interaction to proceed in self-directed groups wherever "it's working."

5. After allowing reasonable time for this partner SCAMPERing, instruct students to reassemble as one group. "Let's get together now and share the outcomes of the SCAMPERed mind maps."

Structured Discussion Using these and other questions, initiate a discussion with your students on the SCAMPER technique and their readiness to write their creative bios. "How did you refine or embellish your brainstormed cluster by SCAMPERing? What is your focus to begin your writing? Do you have novel ideas for formats or approaches? Are you able to visualize the final form you think your writing will take? Is there a dramatic, humorous or clever approach you plan to use to invite the reader into your biographical piece? Are you ready to write?"

Use wait time after each question and response. Encourage thoughtful answers and student-to-student interaction during discussion. As students respond, stand at the opposite side of the room so the comments are projected to the whole group. Keep your eyes on the speaker. If another student chimes in, look at him to direct others toward active listening. If you facilitate group interaction using all of these techniques, the improved quality of your class discussions and verbal interactions will amaze you. Remember, too, to reinforce creative thinking throughout the discussion.

Metacognitive Processing
Promote further and more intimate student processing of the lesson through log entries. Encourage students to make *personal connections* with the new learning and their past experiences. Some lead-ins might be:

> I'm similar to my creative genius because we both . . . .
> (Use a Venn Diagram.)

> I wonder if . . . .

> SCAMPERing a genius is like . . . .

> My problem with SCAMPERing is . . . .

Follow-up
Instead of having students *read* about a creative genius, let them meet and interview a local "genius." Have students prepare interview questions that will allow for in-depth answers and dialogue from people who have a wealth of information to offer. When they get back to class, have students mind map and SCAMPER alone or with a partner the information they gathered.

To introduce the class to their local geniuses, students should SCAMPER—minify, magnify, substitute, etc.—a particular event, quote, trait or piece of information they gathered. Through a quote, play, puppet show, story or any other creative presentation, students should present to the class a glimpse of the interviewee's personality. No one is to present a straight narrative that describes the person's life from birth to present time.

Note: Students should understand that they are not expected to tell the person's whole life story. Students are to use the SCAMPER strategies to develop one aspect, or a small group of aspects, of the person's life—to show the class a bit of that person's unique essence. Presentations are expected to be creative, innovative constructions that prompt other students' curiosity and desire to know more about the people introduced.

Evaluation of Skills:

1. SCAMPER one of the following:

    a. a clothes hanger

    b. an adhesive bandage

    c. a safety pin

    d. a pencil

    e. a blanket

2. Have students complete the following lead-ins in their Thinking Logs:

    To me, creative thinking means . . . .

    I used creative thinking when I . . . .

Critical Thinking
Level II

Analyzing for Bias

Thinking Skill: *Analyzing for Bias*

Everyone is a prisoner of his own experiences. No one can eliminate prejudices—just recognize them.

—Edward R. Murrow

Model Lesson:

Lesson Objective To use critical analysis to determine bias.

Key Vocabulary Bias, exaggeration, charged words, overgeneralization, imbalance, prejudice.

Looking Back In previous lessons, students practiced a deliberate search using the SCAMPER brainstorming technique to promote creative thinking. By applying the SCAMPER guidelines, student-generated ideas were characterized by fluency (quantity) and flexibility (shifts). The focus of the SCAMPER search is divergent in nature. The goal is to facilitate productive creative thinking in students in order to develop a pattern for thinking in a creative mode.

Getting Ready Analyzing data for bias is another type of deliberate search. However, in this case, students conduct a deliberate search of analyses to identify bias or prejudice. The focus of this discriminating search is critical in nature. Its goal is to promote critical, analytical thinking in students to enable them to become discerning consumers of ideas.

Analyzing for bias is a difficult skill to master. Bias is often hidden within the subtleties of written material, under the surface of glossy advertising, or beneath the passion of deeply held beliefs. We are served instant news from all corners of the world as it is still happening. We are bombarded with slick testimonials for a milieu of products. We are witnesses to live political debates that are meticulously manipulated to present the most favorable impressions. We face a deluge of printed material. Newspapers present local and national items that cover a broad scope of interests; magazines highlight particular and varied special-interest topics. In short, we are part and parcel of a media-mania world. How do we know what to believe? What's the proof?—these questions guide students into critical thinking, which includes gathering facts, sorting data, proving or justifying data, and advocating their reasoned conclusions.

Critical thinkers do not believe everything they hear and read. They step back, review the data systematically, look for telling clues through a line-by-line, piece-by-piece search, match clue patterns to an ideal or standard, and make a critical judgment based on the analysis of this data.

Bias is not necessarily a negative component, because it is rooted in belief and conviction:

> *There are only two ways to be quite unprejudiced and impartial. One is to be completely ignorant. The other is to be completely indifferent. Bias and prejudice are attitudes to be kept in hand, not attitudes to be avoided.*
> —Charles P. Curtis

Thus, as critical thinkers, we need to be aware of the possible biases in the material we're exposed to, for only in the thorough examination of data are we able to make judgments based on facts, and advocate opinions based on sound reason.

Bias is the exaggeration of a point of view. It is opinion asserted as fact; it is imbalance, a statement packed with "charged words" or overgeneralizations. Bias is prejudice. Even if that prejudice is unintentional, critical thinkers need to search out all considerations in order to make informed judgments.

At-A-Glance You will initiate development of this concept with a focus activity that asks students to think about a personal bias (a point of view that they represent) and a convincing way to present this viewpoint to others. Next, you will review key vocabulary words. Then you will structure a small-group task to help students develop the concept of point of view or bias and use the concept to

24

analyze data. Finally, you will direct short practices and transfer lessons in which students apply the concept.

Focus Activity

1. Prepare the class for a group brainstorming session by reviewing the DOVE guidelines and eliciting working definitions of *bias* and *point of view*.

2. Instruct students: "Think about a personal bias you may have. Let's compile a list of the points of view we might represent—those perspectives that provide the possibility for bias in our thinking. For example, a *teen-ager* could be one particular viewpoint; *youngest, oldest, middle,* and *only* child are other viewpoints with certain biases. What are some others? Brainstorm as many as you can in five minutes."

3. Next, have students select one viewpoint of bias and verbally present a topic of their choice using that point of view. "For example, if you choose the bias of the *youngest child,* you may argue that young people should have the same bedtime as older siblings; a teen-ager may advocate a no-curfew point of view etc."

Materials Needed

☐ Chalk, eraser and blackboard

☐ BIAS poster

☐ Overhead, screen, projector, transparencies and extension cord

☐ Thinking Log

4. After three or four volunteers have presented their viewpoints, analyze each argument for **bias** clues:

E O I O C	Exaggeration Overgeneralization Imbalance Opinion asserted as fact Charged words

5. Talk about patterns of bias clues that were revealed in the arguments (more than one bias clue). Next, suggest the important search technique called **BIAS**!

Be aware of points of view
Indicate examples of the use of bias clues (EOIOC)
- exaggeration
- overgeneralization
- imbalance
- opinion as fact
- charged words
Account for possible biases by citing proofs
State opinions based on reasoned judgment

6. Using BIAS, critically search the examples students presented for any bias clues they may have missed. Try this exercise several times until students are identifying *clues of bias*. For example:

> Exaggeration - "Never, always . . . ."
> Overgeneralization - "Everyone does!"
> Imbalance - Only one side of the story
> Opinion asserted as fact - "They say . . . ."
> Charged words - "Any idiot knows . . . ."

Activity Objective
To practice basic strategies of analyzing for bias using the tale *The Blind Men and the Elephant.*

Activity
To introduce a new concept it's best to use simple and concrete examples that students can grasp. For that reason, the abstract concept of *bias* is presented in this skill lesson through what may appear to be a very basic level. By beginning at this concrete level, however, you will have a prime example of *bias* (point of view) to refer students to as they progress into the analysis of more subtle and discrete examples.

1. Post the objective and highlight the word *bias* by identifying how viewpoints may cause bias. Provide other examples—such as advertising, political beliefs, special interest groups—that may create bias in what we hear and read.

2. After giving your examples, elicit more examples from students. Remember to encourage responses from different students and to allow time for students to think through or talk through an idea. Display the BIAS poster.

3. To introduce the skill of analyzing for bias, locate a version of the age-old tale *The Blind Men and the Elephant* or retell it in your own words.

Basic story line: *The Blind Men and the Elephant*

1st touched *side* - "It's like a *wall.*"
2nd touched *tail* - "It's like a *rope.*"
3rd touched *tusk* - "It's like a *sword.*"
4th touched *leg* - "It's like a *tree.*"
5th touched *ear* - "It's like a *fan.*"

4. After students have been exposed to the story, ask these questions:

   a. What points of view were presented? Explain why they were so varied.

   b. Give some examples of exaggeration.

   c. How does this story illustrate imbalance?

   d. Why were there so many instances of overgeneralization?

   e. Give some examples of charged words—if you recall any from this story.

   f. Do you think the distortions were intentional? Why or why not?

   g. Does intent in bias make a difference? Why or why not?

   h. In what ways could the blind men investigate differently? Which methods would help validate their ideas?

5. After sufficiently examining the story with these questions, review the BIAS technique and use it in a deliberate search to analyze for bias:

Be aware of points of view.
Indicate examples of the use of bias clues (EOIOC).
Account for possible biases by citing proofs.
State opinion based on reasoned judgment.

Metacognitive Processing
Instruct students to complete one of the following lead-ins in their Thinking Logs. (Use overhead.)

An example of bias is . . . .

A way I could use what I've learned today is . . . .

About bias, I wonder . . . .

In the future . . . .

Discuss as a class. Wrap around the room to elicit entries.

Short Practices:

Lots of short practices in finding *bias clues* help students develop a *pattern for thinking* analytically about bias and prejudice. With this practice, students begin to question, through a *deliberate search*, the mountain of claims made by the media. In addition, they will begin to recognize their own prejudices as they analyze and evaluate information critically. In time, they will become critical thinkers who base their judgments on fact and reason rather than on undetected bias.

■ Place this figure on the chalkboard

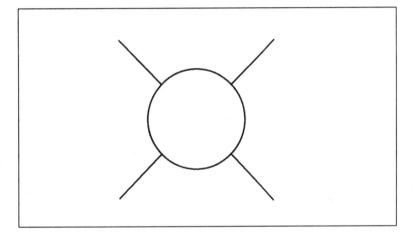

Mentally divide the class into three groups, giving each group a set of cards with one of the following directions written on them:

Directions

> **Group 1**—Use the design and visualize an object coming STRAIGHT AT YOU: Draw your idea.

> **Group 2**—Use the design and visualize an object DIRECTLY ABOVE YOU: Draw your idea.

> **Group 3**—Use the design and visualize an object DIRECTLY BENEATH YOU: Draw your idea.

Instruct students: "Read your directions, but do not discuss them with anyone. Make your sketches privately. Get started, now. You'll have about 10 minutes."

After students have completed their drawings, ask them to tape their drawings onto the wall. Allow time for students to observe the drawings. Next, process the idea of how *different points of view* can influence our perspectives (and drawings). Some leading questions might be: "We all looked at the same model. Why do we have such diverse drawings? Can you identify particular points of view? Which ones are most appropriate to the data presented? Why? Does everyone agree? Why or Why not? What is the ideal? What is the standard?" Allow ample time for reflection and discussion.

After the discussion, review key vocabulary—bias, prejudice, exaggeration, overgeneralization, imbalance, opinion, charged words—and have students make a Thinking Log entry using these lead-ins:

> Different points of view . . . .
>
> I never . . . .
>
> An example of bias that I know is . . . .

■ Examples of bias are readily available in advertisements. As students begin to analyze for bias, have them use old magazines, TV, and radio ads to find bias clues. Prepare a bulletin board or poster for students to refer to as a cue to the bias clues:

E	Exaggeration
O	Overgeneralization
I	Imbalance
O	Opinion asserted as fact
C	Charged words

Using magazine and news articles, again, have students read critically for bias clues. Also, have them conduct the BIAS search:

> **B**e aware of points of view, predict.
> **I**ndicate examples of the use of bias clues and EOIOC.
> **A**ccount for possible bias clues by citing proofs.
> **S**tate an opinion based on your reasoned judgment.

Key Vocabulary

- *Exaggeration:* "Never, always...."

- *Overgeneralization:* "Everyone does!"

- *Imbalance:* Only one side of the story

- *Opinion asserted as fact:* "They say...."

- *Charged words:* "Any idiot knows...."

■ Role-Play: Stage an incident or accident in front of the class. Assign points of view and have students relate their version of the incident *from that point of view*. Analyze for clues of bias after all viewpoints have been expressed.

Or, tell the roles assigned and have students *predict* the *bias* for each point of view. *Prediction* is an important aspect of analyzing for bias. As we read and listen critically, we should be aware of the 'point of viewing' and the *possible bias* that may be present.

Transfer Lesson:
Social Studies/ Current Events

Analyzing for Bias
BIAS Technique

- **B**e aware of points of view.

- **I**ndicate spottings of bias clues (EOIOC).

- **A**ccount for possible bias by citing proofs.

- **S**tate an opinion based on your reasoned judgment.

Focus Activity Distribute copies of a current newspaper's lead article. Instruct students to read the article. In their Thinking Logs, have students complete a lead-in about the article:

Several points of view that could be represented are . . . .

The author seems to . . . .

Use the whiparound technique to sample the log entries. Remember to enforce the DOVE guidelines and honor the students' right to pass. Give a "Hurrah!" to each contributor.

Objective To practice analyzing material for bias by detecting points of view.

Activity

1. Divide the class into groups of four. The tallest person will be discussion leader, the shortest person will be recorder, the second tallest person will be the materials manager and the third tallest person will be the timekeeper.

2. Tell students: "You will have two tasks in your groups. First, analyze the existing article for possible bias using the BIAS technique. Record your findings on large paper.

3. "Second, rewrite the headline and the lead sentence to *flagrantly* represent a biased point of view. You may select what the point of view will be.

4. "Write your new headline and lead sentence on large paper. When you have completed both tasks, post your sheets on the wall. You will have 15 minutes for this activity.

5. "Show thumbs up if you understand the directions, thumbs down if you have a question." Elicit clarification from other students to help those who indicate confusion, then let the groups get started.

6. After 15 minutes, have the straggler groups finish and prepare for the *Structured Discussion*.

Structured Discussion
When all groups have posted their worksheets, let the group observers explain the findings listed on their BIAS sheets. Continue until all groups have reacted. Allow time for students to explore in depth the analysis of bias. Next, using the sheets with the biased headlines, instruct students to jot down on notebook paper the probable point of view each group used as the group's observer reads the headline and the lead sentence. After all groups have presented their bias sheets, discuss their evaluations. As students report their answers, elicit justification through the BIAS technique. For example, for the point of view they think is being represented with the bias, they should *prove* the bias by identifying EOIOC evidence on the sheet.

Metacognitive Processing
Instruct students to complete in their Thinking Logs one of these lead-ins:

In this lesson, I discovered . . . .

Bias is both good and bad because . . . .

Follow-up
Using the same procedures suggested in the previous newspaper activity, have students detect biases in textbook units. Have them rewrite a boldfaced heading and lead-in sentence with a biased viewpoint. Share the student work and identify bias through BIAS analysis.

For example:

■ During a unit on the Civil War, have students write down causes of the war from different points of view:

   a. African-American slave
   b. Yankee general
   c. Northern manufacturer
   d. Southern plantation owner
   e. Young recruit from the North

■ During a Science unit on ecology, have students consider these points of view:

    a. Farmer
    b. Amusement park owner
    c. Hunter
    d. Conservationist
    e. Biologist

Transfer Lesson:
Social Studies/ Government and Law

Focus Activity Using a well-known fairy tale such as *The Three Little Pigs* elicit a retelling of the tale by students. After refreshing students' memories with the "facts" of the story, give these instructions: "B.D. Wolf is coming to trial. He has been indicted on three counts—property destruction, vandalism, and public disturbance. Your job today is to select an unbiased jury to hear the case. Those of you on this side of the room will vote on possible jurors. Those of you on that side of the room will be assigned roles to play in the legal proceedings."

Objective To practice analyzing for bias through the simulation of a jury selection.

Activity

1. Hand out cards defining the various roles. Since the attorneys are key to the proceedings, select those roles carefully, choosing students who can ad-lib and carry on quite well in this sort of simulation.

    Defense Attorney: You will represent B. D. Wolf.

    State-Appointed Prosecutor: You will represent the Pigs' family.

    Judge: You will preside over the proceedings.

    Educator: You teach the little piggies.

    Lady Skunk: Animal kingdom always shuns you.

    Cab Driver: You, too live in a small cottage.

    Bank President: The piggies need a loan to rebuild.

    Land Baron: You want the piggies' land.

    Local Contractor: You might get the job to rebuild the houses.

High-Rise Dweller: You can't relate to "cottage" dwellers.

Bailiff: You keep order and escort the prospects in and out of the room.

Court Recorder: You write down the proceedings.

Court Reporter: You're looking for a story.

Court Clerk: You swear in prospective jurors and say "all rise" as the judge enters.

Policeman: You are on the police force in another town.

Other:

2. **Instructions to the defense attorney and the prosecutor:** "You will ask questions of prospective jurors to determine the possible biases. You may use the next few minutes to formulate your questions."

3. **Instructions to the role players out in the hall:** "You will use as many bias clues as you can while being interviewed. *Exaggerate! Oversimplify!* Show an *imbalance* in your feelings about things that might show bias on the case. Assert *opinion* as fact and use emotionally *charged* words. Remember, you have a role to play. Do not let your personal feelings enter into the role playing. Represent the point of view of your assigned role. Think about your role and its appropriate viewpoints while I give the others their instructions."

4. **Instructions to the audience, while prospective jurors are out of the room:** "Those of you who will be voting on jurors have a difficult task. Your *goal* is to select *six* jurors. Your criteria is simply to find those candidates who you feel demonstrate the *least bias* toward the case. You will use the Bias Clue Sheet as you listen to the proceedings. (See Bias Clue Sheet.)

"Each time a prospective juror reveals a bias clue during the selection proceedings or via his suspected point of view, make a mark in the proper box. For example, if the cabbie describes his twig house that he has slaved for all his life, you might mark *charged words* because of the emotional word *slaved*: A bias for the pigs' predicament is suspected. You may want to make notes on the side of the sheet for later reference.

"At the end of the selection process, the six characters with the lowest score will be selected. However, either attorney can reject any prospective juror."

BIAS CLUE SHEET CLUES	Example	Lady Skunk	Cab Driver	Bank President	Land Baron	Local Contractor	High-Rise Dweller	Educator	Policeman	Other	Other	NOTES
Exaggeration												
Overgeneralization												
Imbalance												
Opinion as Fact												
Charged Words												
TOTALS												

Bias Clue Sheet

5. **Instructions to the court personnel in the room:** "You are playing the roles of people who work in the courts. Be professional, assume the identity of your role and act accordingly. Any questions?"

6. **Instructions for role playing: Jury Selection**

   "The prospective jurors are called to the stand and are interviewed by both attorneys. Either attorney can reject a prospective juror. If a juror is rejected, *no* reason is given and the person is dismissed at that time."

   Ironical note: Each attorney develops a "bias profile" of jurors he feels will be most *sympathetic to his client's point of view.* As he interviews, he is actually looking for *particular bias* under the guise of interviewing for *no* bias.

7. Rearrange the room as needed. Reassemble all students back in the room and begin the proceedings. Question all the prospective jurors, using the simulated court procedures. Use the role definitions as guides to courtroom behaviors.

   After the final candidate is interviewed, each student tallies his Bias Clue Sheet.

Structured Discussion Now, do a class tally of the Bias Clue Sheets. Remember, the *six* characters with the *smallest* numbers tallied are the jurors selected by the unbiased audience— even if some of those same people have been dismissed by the attorneys.

Lead a class discussion about the simulation. Elicit multiple answers. Practice wait time. Here are some suggested discussion questions:

How was bias most frequently revealed? (EOIOC)

Is it possible to be a totally unbiased juror?

How do attorneys finally select the jurors? How do they weigh the criteria?

Describe some *nonverbal* clues of bias.

Who appeared most *flagrantly* biased? Why do you think so? What clues did you detect?

Who appeared most *unbiased* of all? Why?

Describe a profile of bias from the state attorney's point of view . . . and the defense attorney's point of view.

Metacognitive Processing Write a Thinking Log
entry about *bias:*

A *positive* aspect of *bias* is . . . .

A *negative* aspect of *bias* is . . . .

An *intriguing* aspect of *bias* is . . . .

Follow-up By practicing the BIAS technique, students can
advocate their conclusions. (See page 29 for a review of BIAS.)

Using the Human Graph for charting bias/no bias, have students

- analyze famous quotes for possible bias.

- analyze television speeches, news stories, and "topic" shows for bias.

- analyze television shows for bias; recognize the points of view and the *point* the show is making.

- analyze the lyrics of favorite "hits" for possible bias.

To use *The Human Graph* as a teaching strategy, simply stand in the center of the room and have students cluster in front of you. Draw an imaginary line dividing the space into segments or actually place masking tape on the floor with the appropriate markings. Assign *degrees of agreement* to different portions of the graph. Students can indicate the intensity of their convictions by standing in the assigned areas. (See The Human Graph on next page.)

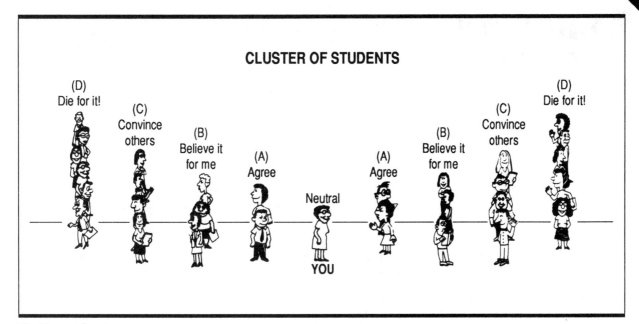

CLUSTER OF STUDENTS

(D) Die for it! (C) Convince others (B) Believe it for me (A) Agree Neutral YOU (A) Agree (B) Believe it for me (C) Convince others (D) Die for it!

The Human Graph

Pose a question as you indicate the ends of the graph corresponding to each answer: "Would you rather _____ or _____? Or do you think _____ or _____?" Watch as students move to one side or the other. Then ask why they moved there. LISTEN! Permit time for a student to explain his decision. WAIT! Let him fully develop the depth of his thoughts as he discovers the *connection* between his decision and his experiences. Allow movement along the graph as students change their minds, but also encourage students to *advocate* their *opinions* and to demonstrate *conviction* in their *beliefs*. Continue to move through the graph in a similar manner, sampling as many ideas as time permits.

As The Human Graph evolves, be aware of and discuss with the students (a) how quickly one reaches a decision, (b) how far to a side one moves, (c) how often one changes her mind, (d) how one comes to her decision, (e) how one reacts in a minority/majority position, and (f) how one reflects her attitudes in her choices.

Remember, through the interactive nature of *critical analysis* and *creative synthesis*, decisions are made, convictions are crystallized, beliefs are solidified, and actions are taken. Decisions are made moment by moment. Let's experience and examine the processes with students. First, let's get them to think. Then, let's get them to think about their thinking. Let's give them opportunities to ponder patterns for thinking. Finally, as teachers, let's take advantage of those "teachable moments."

Evaluation of Skills:

1. List some bias clues.

2. Read this quote and analyze it for bias clues using the BIAS technique.

   The enemy is flesh and blood human beings hiding behind the veil of corporate bigness and anonymity.

3. Write a brief argument with a personal bias evidenced.

Thinking For Problem Solving Level II

Creative Problem-Solving

Thinking Skill:

Creative Problem-Solving

We have in our thinkery, a well-exercised power to think ourselves out of trials and difficulties.

—F. Robley Feland

Model Lesson:

Lesson Objective To identify through practice the elements of a creative problem-solving process.

Key Vocabulary Fact, problem, solution, challenge, criteria, diverge, converge, PNI.

Looking Back In previous lessons, students used creative thinking patterns in the SCAMPER brainstorming techniques. Their critical thinking patterns were exercised while analyzing for bias. Students discovered that a *deliberate search*, either for creative divergence or critical convergence, is a systematic method that helps "cover all the bases" in a comprehensive manner.

Getting Ready *You need a ride to the track meet. You have two best friends with birthday parties on the same day. You ruined your brother's favorite tape. You have TONS of homework. What do you do?* Pose this problem to your students and typically, their problem-solving solutions will fall into a sequence something like this:

1. Think of choices and alternatives.
2. Rate/rank choices according to perceived outcomes.
3. Decide!
4. Take action!

You see, students solve problems like these all the time—we *all* solve problems like these all the time. Somehow, instinctively, we manage to figure our way out of messy situations. In fact, we do it so automatically that usually we never think about *how* we solve our problems. Yet, we know that we think about possible choices and somehow decide on a course of action.

The fact is, the human race is a resourceful lot. We are ingenious when circumstances call for ingenuity, even if we do fumble about in our own hit-or-miss, random manner. We do manage!

The point is that someone has taken the initiative to jot down this somewhat random path we all seem to follow in solving life's problems. In fact, Alex Osborn, and later, Sidney Parnes, identified key components to the problem-solving process and outlined deliberate steps to take to develop effective *patterns for thinking* in problem-solving situations.

The creative problem-solving model illustrates the dual ways the thinking mind "searches" or "scans" a problem. It approaches a problem with the deliberate search techniques of creative ideation to generate alternatives and critical analysis, and to develop criteria for evaluation. Both divergent productive thinking and convergent evaluative thinking comprise mindful problem solving. This dual nature of our search patterns is illustrated in the Creative Problem-Solving Flowsheet, an adaptation and contraction of the Osborn-Parnes model which teachers have found effective for students in their early exposure to that model. (See the Creative Problem-Solving Flowsheet on next page.)

We *diverge* to gather all the facts; then, we *converge* on the real problem. We engage in creative ideation to accumulate a list of alternatives; then, we critically analyze those choices based on some criteria. We generate solutions and evaluate them for the best one as we speculate on the acceptance of our plan of action. Then, we face the new challenges of implementation and the cycle begins again.

The experienced problem solver is comfortable with both creative and critical patterns for thinking and knows how to use them alternately (and at times almost simultaneously) as he or she tackles perplexing situations.

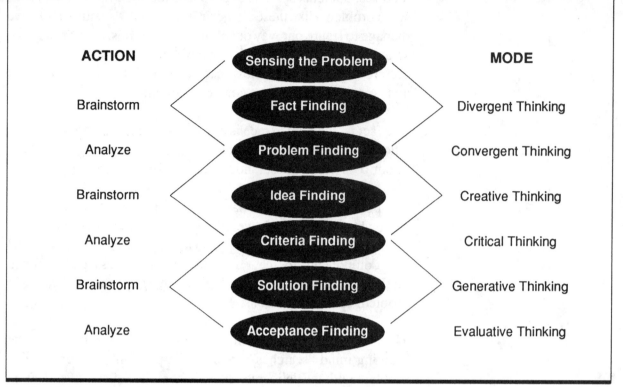

ACTION		MODE
	Sensing the Problem	
Brainstorm	Fact Finding	Divergent Thinking
Analyze	Problem Finding	Convergent Thinking
Brainstorm	Idea Finding	Creative Thinking
Analyze	Criteria Finding	Critical Thinking
Brainstorm	Solution Finding	Generative Thinking
Analyze	Acceptance Finding	Evaluative Thinking

Creative Problem-Solving Flowsheet*

Edward de Bono, founder of the CoRT Thinking Skills Program, tells an anecdote that illustrates the benefits of adapting *deliberate* patterns for thinking about problems: In a new high-rise, employees are disgruntled because of the constant aggravation of having to wait for an elevator. After a group brainstorming session, one suggestion that came up for later analysis was an idea that had initially seemed way off base, totally out of context with the problem at hand.

Someone suggested during the brainstorming that mirrors could be installed on the walls around the elevators. The reasoning was that if people were preoccupied (looking at themselves) they wouldn't notice the wait for the elevator. Ultimately, this solution proved not only cost-effective, but client-effective too! Creative ideation and critical evaluation are viable patterns for thinking in problem-solving situations.

At-A-Glance You will begin development of the creative problem-solving process with a focus activity that invites students to describe a personal problem. Next, you will ask students to voluntarily share some of their issues that are relevant to many other students. After introducing the creative problem-solving model, cooperative groups will use the model as they practice on the previously shared student problems. Short practices will be applied to newspaper advice columns. Finally, transfer lessons in which students apply the creative problem-solving model directly to content areas will be implemented.

Focus Activity

Materials Needed

- ☐ Poster of CPS Flowsheet

- ☐ Transparencies of Traffic Jam Statement and Traffic Jam Charts I & II

- ☐ Overhead projector

- ☐ Butcher paper, markers, and tape

- ☐ Numbered cards

- ☐ Chalk, eraser, and blackboard

- ☐ Thinking Logs

1. To set the climate for meaningful problem solving, begin by sharing with the class a personal problem you've faced and the subsequent outcome of that situation. Next, place this message, adapted from Marilyn Burns' *The Book of Think*, on an overhead transparency:

> **Traffic Jam Statement**
>
> Once I had a problem twice my size.   It was about _____. Believe me, it caused a terrible traffic jam in my head. I couldn't decide if I _____ or _____. Then, _____.
>
> Probably, what helped most was _____ _____. Now, when I have a REAL HUMDINGER OF A PROBLEM, I _____. It _____ _____.

2. After students have had ample time to respond to the paragraphs and to reflect on a problem, post two large, *long* sheets of butcher paper on the wall.

TRAFFIC JAMS	STRATEGIES USED
1. Two dates	1. Avoidance (left town)
2.	2.

Responding in turn and following the DOVE guidelines, each student should relate 1) his or her *problem* and 2) his or her *solution* using That's a Good Idea. (See next page.)

That's a Good Idea—Guidelines

Record a student's answer on the proper sheet.

The next person in turn says, "That's a good idea because _____."

Then, that same student says, "My problem was _____. I solved it by _____."

The third student in turn says, "That's a good idea because _____," and then states his or her problem and solution.

The process continues around the room until you have recorded a problem and strategy for each student. (These Traffic Jams will be used throughout this Creative Problem-Solving unit.)

Activity Objective
To practice creative and critical patterns for thinking in problem-solving situations.

Activity

1. Elicit examples of *creative thinking* from the list of posted strategies used by students. Have students justify their chosen strategy to illustrate the *critical thinking* component that is inherent in their final solutions. For example, with the traffic jam of two birthday parties, the *avoidance* strategy eliminated the possibility of one friend's feelings being hurt because the problem solver avoided disclosure of the problem. Show the Creative Problem-solving Flowsheet on the overhead to explain the critical-creative thinking process. Discuss the components of the model.

2. Next, divide the class into groups of four, with a materials manager, discussion leader, recorder, and observer/timekeeper.

3. Demonstrate a finished newsprint model as you give the task instructions for the next activity in this lesson. Each group should conclude with a list that has a format similar to the Sample Traffic Jam shown on the next page. Remember to emphasize the basic steps of the process.

4. "We are going to use deliberate creative and critical patterns for thinking to handle a traffic jam. Each manager must select a

SAMPLE TRAFFIC JAM USING THE
CREATIVE PROBLEM-SOLVING MODEL

« GATHER FACTS »

(state "mess")
Two birthday parties on same day.
Both are my best friends!
Like both; don't want to
hurt feelings.

» STATE PROBLEM «

Keep both as friends.

« GENERATE IDEAS »
(Think SCAMPER)

Go to both for a little while.
Pick only one party to go to.
Forget it!
Send gifts, but don't go to
either party.
Write Dear Abby.
Confess! Tell them my problem.

» ANALYZE «
FOR BEST 3

(1) Pick only one party.
(2) Send gifts, don't go to either party.
(3) Confess! Tell them my problem.

Alternatives	P (+)	N (-)	I
(1) Pick one party	Keep one friend.	Lose other friend?	Could find out who's my best friend.
(2) Send gifts. Go to neither party.	Good compromise.	Have to buy two gifts.	Could go to the ball game that day.
(3) Confess! Tell them my problem.	No guilt, they might decide for me.	They might get mad.	I might get sympathy votes for honesty.

« EVALUATE »

P-Positive
N-Negative
I-Intriguing

» RATIONALE «

Hope for Understanding

» PLAN OF ACTION «

Confess

« » = Divergent thinking   » « = Convergent thinking

number from this set of cards." Have numbers that correspond to the number of Traffic Jam problems in the Focus Activity. For example, if you had 30 student problems, you need cards numbered from 1 to 30.

5. "The number tells you which traffic jam your group will tackle. Recorders should state the traffic jam at the top of the group's worksheet.

6. "Using the DOVE guidelines and response-in-turn, complete your chart using my example of two birthday parties as a reference. I will be wandering around if you need help. Are there any questions about the task?

7. "Remember, as the model *diverges* you will need to think in a fluent, creative mode; as the model *converges*, you will need to think analytically in a critical mode. Both patterns of thinking are necessary in problem-solving situations. Your creative problem solving of the Traffic Jams will be due at the end of the period. Go ahead and get started."

8. During the next class period, allow a few minutes for groups to review and revise their creative/critical solutions to their Traffic Jams. Instruct managers to post the completed charts in the room.

9. Have the observer/timekeepers present their charts to the class. As the problem statement and final solution (plan of action) are stated, record them on two sheets posted next to the two original Traffic Jam sheets from yesterday's Focus Activity—Traffic Jams and Strategies Used. (Only one-fourth of the original list of traffic jams will have been used!) Continue this process until all groups have reported. Allow time for interaction as enthusiastic tales unfold about finding that "final solution." Students will be excited about their thinking! See the sample charts below.

Sample Traffic Jam Charts

TRAFFIC JAMS	STRATEGIES USED	PROBLEM STATEMENTS	CHOSEN SOLUTIONS
1. Two birthday parties	1. Talk to friends	1. Keep both friends	1. Confess
2. Lots of homework	2. Didn't do it	2. (not solved by a group)	2. (not solved by a group)
3.	3.	3.	3.

10. Use this question to whip around the classroom and elicit reactions to the process: What was most interesting about the problem-solving process? Continue around the group, encouraging personal responses, but accepting, "I pass," as always.

Metacognitive Processing
Instruct students to use one of the following lead-ins for a Thinking Log entry:

> A personal problem similar to the one my group processed is _____.
>
> I wonder . . . .
>
> I never realized . . . .

After completing the log entry, have students turn to a partner. Instruct them to share PNI statements on problem solving.

Short Practices:

Frequent, guided, short practices make learning permanent! Offer your students the chance to become fluent problem solvers every day and encourage them to practice their problem-solving skills at home and at school with these short practices.

■ Using collected (and selected) columns similar to Dear Abby's, instruct students to work with a partner to complete the guide below and to assist Dear Abby in her advice column.

"Mess":

Facts:

Real Problem:

(SCAMPER) Ideas:

PNI 3 Solutions:

	+	–	I
1.			
2.			
3.			

Plan of Action (advice): _____
_____.

■ Using cartoons or comics—for example, "Calvin and Hobbes" and the "Far Side"—have students solve the problems of their favorite cartoon characters. They'll have a laugh and come up with some creative solutions as well. Have students use the guide from the previous Short Practice activity.

Transfer Lesson:
Stop Action/ Instant Replays or Changing the Course of History

Focus Activity In your Thinking Log, complete one of the following lead-ins:

The focus of our (social studies) history class was . . . .

One historical problem that emerged was . . . .

Objective To practice creative and critical patterns for thinking with the Creative Problem-Solving Flowsheet.

Activity

1. "Using an event in history, a real problem situation that we've read about, we're going to use the concepts of stop action and instant replay. In other words, if we could stop the action and replay the event with a novel and innovative solution, how might history be rewritten? Our 'instant replay' will be our new version based on the outcomes of our creative problem-solving process."

   A concrete example will clarify. *"What if*, the colonists had used creative problem-solving with their taxation problem? Could they have avoided a 'bloody war' by generating alternative actions? That's the kind of exercise we're going to do. We're going to 'change the course of history,' but first we need to know the facts as they are."

2. "Using your Thinking Log entries, let's list some perplexing situations that we've recently read about." List all the items on the board.

3. "In groups of four, with a leader, manager, recorder, and timekeeper, apply the Creative Problem-Solving Flowsheet to one of these historical situations we have listed on the board." Selection should be random. Use numbers to choose. Use the same procedure you used in the Traffic Jam lesson. Review the

creative-critical (expanding-contracting) model. Post the example problem of the two birthday parties from the Traffic Jam lesson. "You will have the remainder of the class time. At the end of the period, please have your completed chart ready to post. We'll *relive* history through the *rewritings*, during our next class."

4. Facilitate groups as needed.

Structured Discussion
Again, using the posted charts, have group observers relay their historical replays. Encourage lively discussion—after all, you are changing the course of history through creative and critical patterns for thinking. Sparked by the novel outcomes speculated, students will automatically generate more "what ifs" that can become material for future Stop Action/Instant Replay activities.

Metacognitive Processing
Have students complete these log lead-ins:

Solving problems of history . . . .

I'm learning to . . . .

The problem about _____ makes me think of _____.

Follow-up
Videotape skits of Stop Action/Instant Replays as you witness "history in the making."

Transfer Lesson:
Literature/ "A Novel Idea"

Focus Activity Introduce students to this lesson, "A Novel Idea," by forming "book groups" of four students. Each book group will need a discussion leader, materials manager, recorder, and observer/timekeeper.

Obtain multiple copies of several different age-appropriate paperback novels. Briefly, preview the themes of each novel and have groups select the one they will read in their groups.

Distribute copies of the books and invite students to browse through them. Assign *one* chapter for tomorrow.

Objective To practice creative and critical thinking with the Creative Problem-Solving Flowsheet.

Activity Using novels, lead students into predicting outcomes based on the critical-creative model. Predicting what will happen next not only heightens students' motivation to "read on," but it also enhances comprehension for students who are required to "read with rigor," while they think critically and creatively.

When the groups meet next, explain to students the objective, the role responsibilities, and the task.

1. "The objective today is to practice creative problem solving in your book groups."

2. Show the role responsibilities on an overhead.

   a. **Leader:** Elicits probable perplexing situations that are developing in the storyline to date.

   b. **Manager:** Gathers facts from the group about the problem that is developing and defines a *manageable* problem by writing a simple problem statement. The leader may elicit further clarification from the group.

   c. **Recorder:** Records the problem, facts, and problem statement.

   d. **Observer/Timekeeper:** Observes the group process. Using skills of *observation*, the observer begins the brainstorming and lists ideas that *could* develop based on the facts and problems presented. This person records all of the ideas stated. Go for quantity.

3. "Your groups will have 20 minutes to produce this information." Show a sample prediction sheet. Facilitate groups as needed, encouraging and reinforcing role responsibilities and evidence of critical and creative thinking.

Sample Predictions

Novel: (Title and Author)

"Mess":

Problem Statement:

Predictions: (Ideas)

---

4. After 20 minutes, have groups review their lists of predictions by having the person who suggested the idea state evidence, the *proof* in the book's passages, or *interpretations* and *inferences*.

5. Vote and decide by consensus what the group thinks will happen next as a probable outcome of the problem situation identified. Allow ample time for groups to interact. Reinforce evidences of students thinking as problem solvers.

Structured Discussion Call all groups together. *Do not* try to discuss the various novels in progress. Use this time to talk about *prediction* and how the Creative Problem-Solving Flowsheet is a useful tool for developing reading sophistication. (Plus, it's just fun to try to "outguess" the author!) Good thinkers use prediction frequently. For an excellent discussion starter, whip around the classroom with this lead-in:

Predicting outcomes is similar to _____ because . . . .

After accepting responses in turn from around the room, you might facilitate further discussion with some of these questions:

What do authors do to build suspense?

How might you adapt some of these techniques in your writing?

How might creative problem solving help you develop a piece of writing?

At the beginning of the next period, prove the predictions through selected readings in the book groups. Proceed from that point with a new chart each time the groups meet. See if predictions improve in accuracy or if students' predictions would actually make a better story . . . then lead them into writing their creative story plots.

Metacognitive Processing
Have students make an entry in their Thinking Logs using one of these lead-ins:

The problem my book group identified reminded me of . . . .

My predicted outcome is _____ because . . . .

Creative problem solving seems . . . .

Follow-up
Students can practice using their skill in predicting outcomes by using creative problem solving with TV shows. Also, this is a natural lead-in to mysteries and tales of the unknown.

Evaluation of Skills:

1. Explain how both creative and critical patterns for thinking apply to the Creative Problem-Solving Flowsheet.

2. List the steps typically applied in creative problem solving.

3. Brainstorm a list of ten or more issues currently in the news that are "perplexing situations." (Pick ones for which creative problem solving apply!)

4. Use at least five of these words in a paragraph about problem solving: acceptance, ideas, challenge, ideation, facts, divergence, solution, convergence, problem, criteria.

Keep Them Thinking Level II

Masters Appendix

Premise 1

The teacher is the architect of the intellect.

A teacher affects eternity. He never knows where his influence ends.
—Henry Adams

Premise 2

The student is the capable apprentice.

'Come to the edge,' he said.
They said, 'We are afraid.'
'Come to the edge,' he said. They came.
He pushed them . . . and they flew.
—Apollinaire

Premise 3

Thinking is more basic than the basics— it frames all learning.

Intelligent behavior is knowing what to do when you don't know what to do.
—Arthur Costa

Elements of Creativity

❑ Fluency – quantity

❑ Flexibility – shifts

❑ Elaboration – detail

❑ Originality – uniqueness

DOVE Rules for Brainstorming

Defer judgment

Opt for original and off-beat

Vast numbers are important

Expand on ideas by hitchhiking

"In a hole in the ground,

there lived a hobbit.

Not a nasty, dirty, wet hole, filled with

ends of worms and an oozy smell,

nor yet a dry, bare, sandy hole

with nothing in it to sit down on or to eat;

it was a hobbit-hole,

and that means comfort."

—J.R.R. Tolkien
The Hobbit

SCAMPER

Substitute

Combine

Adapt

Modify, magnify, or minify

Put to other uses

Eliminate or elaborate

Reverse, rearrange

SCAMPER Prompters

SUBSTITUTE: Who else instead? What else instead? Other ingredient? Other material? Other process? Other power? Other place? Other approach? Other tone of voice?

COMBINE: How about a blend, an assortment, an ensemble? Combine units? Combine purposes? Combine appeals? Combine ideas?

ADAPT: What else is like this? What other idea does this suggest? Does something in the past offer a parallel? What could I copy? Whom could I emulate?

MODIFY: New twist? Change meaning, color, motion, sound, order, form, shape?

    MAGNIFY: What to add? More time? Greater frequency? Stronger? Higher? Longer? Thicker? Extra Value? Plus ingredient? Duplicate? Multiply? Exaggerate?

    MINIFY: Smaller? Condensed? Miniature? Lower? Shorter? Lighter? Split up? Understate?

PUT TO OTHER USES: New ways to use as is? Other uses if modified?

ELIMINATE: Omit? What to subtract?

REVERSE: How about opposites? Turn it backward? Turn it upside down? Reverse roles? Change shoes? Turn tables? Turn other cheek?

    REARRANGE: Interchange components? Other pattern? Other layout? Other sequence? Transpose cause and effect? Change pace? Change schedule?

Hex Message

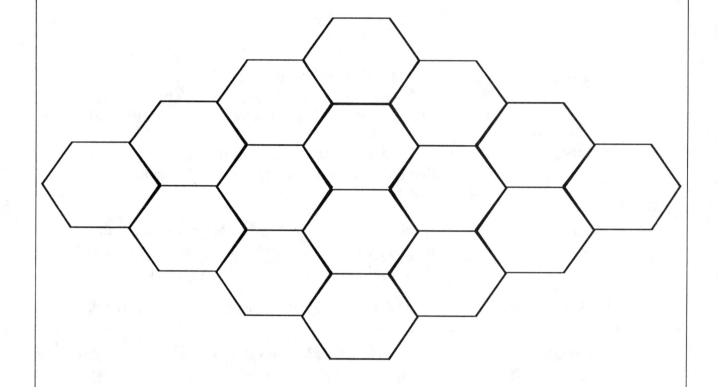

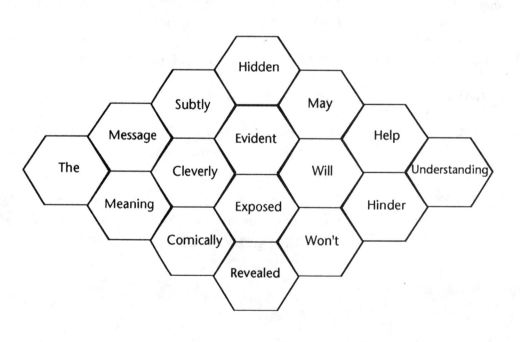

What is the day after the day after tomorrow, if the day before the day before yesterday was Monday?

A man buys a horse for $50 and sells it for $60. He buys the horse back for $70 and then sells it again for $80. Did he earn or lose money, and how much? Or did he come out even?

Mind Map Model

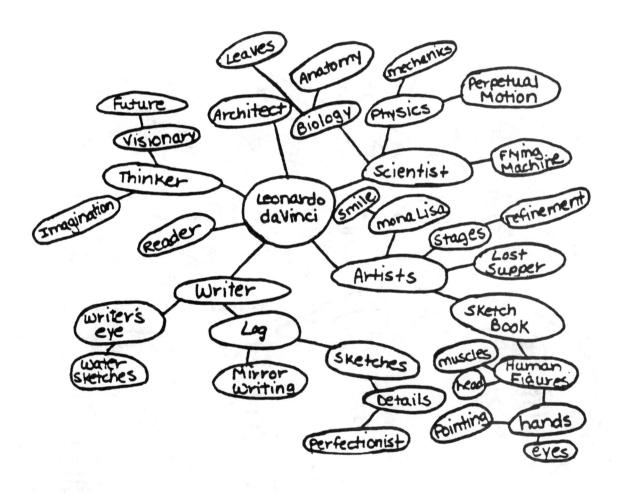

SCAMPERed Mind Map
(minified)

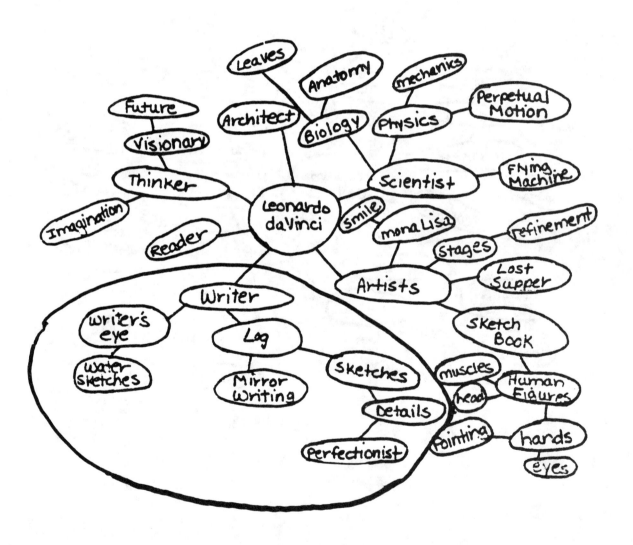

"There are only two ways to be quite unprejudiced and impartial. One is to be completely ignorant. The other is to be completely indifferent. Bias and prejudice are attitudes to be kept in hand, not attitudes to be avoided."

—Charles P. Curtis

E Exaggeration

O Overgeneralization

I Imbalance

O Opinion asserted as fact

C Charged words

EOIOC Examples

Exaggeration

"Never, always...."

Overgeneralization

"Everyone does!"

Imbalance

Only one side of the story

Opinion asserted as fact

"They say...."

Charged words

"Any idiot knows...."

BIAS

Be aware of points of view

Indicate spottings of bias clues

(EOIOC)

Account for possible bias by

citing proofs

State an opinion based on your

reasoned judgment

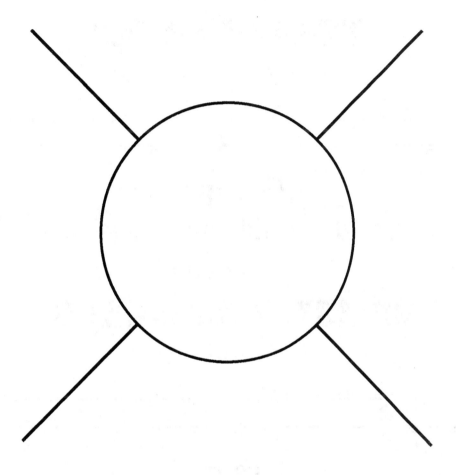

Group 1

Use the design and visualize
an object coming

STRAIGHT AT YOU.

Draw your idea.

Group 2

Use the design and visualize
an object coming

DIRECTLY ABOVE YOU.

Draw your idea.

Group 3

Use the design and visualize
an object coming

DIRECTLY BENEATH YOU.

Draw your idea.

Bias Clue Sheet

NOTES						
CLUES	Exaggeration	Overgeneralization	Imbalance	Opinion as Fact	Charged Words	TOTALS

The Human Graph

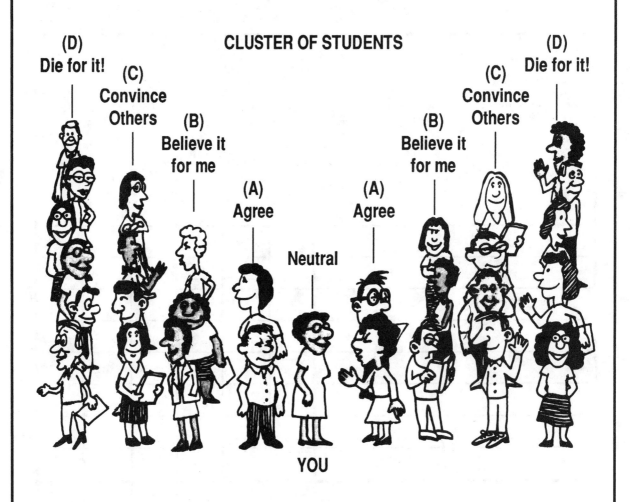

CLUSTER OF STUDENTS

(D)
Die for it!

(C)
Convince
Others

(B)
Believe it
for me

(A)
Agree

Neutral

(A)
Agree

(B)
Believe it
for me

(C)
Convince
Others

(D)
Die for it!

YOU

Creative Problem-Solving Flowsheet

ACTION		MODE
	Sensing the Problem	
Brainstorm	Fact Finding	Divergent Thinking
Analyze	Problem Finding	Convergent Thinking
Brainstorm	Idea Finding	Creative Thinking
Analyze	Criteria Finding	Critical Thinking
Brainstorm	Solution Finding	Generative Thinking
Analyze	Acceptance Finding	Evaluative Thinking

Traffic Jam Statement

Once I had a problem twice my size. It was about _____. Believe me, it caused a terrible traffic jam in my head. I couldn't decide if I _____ or _____. Then, _____.

Probably, what helped most was _____. Now, when I have a REAL HUMDINGER OF A PROBLEM, I _____. It _____ _____.

The process continues around the room until everyone has completed the statements.

That's a Good Idea—Guidelines

Record each answer on the proper sheet.

The next person in turn says, "That's a good idea because _____."

Then, that same student says, "My problem was _____. I solved it by _____."

Then the next student in turn says, "That's a good idea because _____," and then states his problem and solution.

Evaluating Solutions

Alternatives	P (+)	N (−)	I

Traffic Jam Charts I

TRAFFIC JAMS	STRATEGIES USED

Traffic Jam Charts II

PROBLEM STATEMENTS	OPTED SOLUTIONS

Problem-Solving Chart

"Mess":

Facts:

Real Problem:

(SCAMPER) ideas:

PNI 3 Solutions:

	+	−	I
1. 2. 3.			

Plan of Action (advice): _____

_____

Worksheet Model for Original Lessons

To assist you in creating your own thinking lessons that follow the model explained in the introduction, we have included a blank worksheet which outlines the major components. Feel free to photocopy these worksheet pages. Fill them in with your own lesson content to tailor thinking lessons specifically to the needs of your class.

Lesson Objective

Key Vocabulary

Looking Back

Getting Ready

At-A-Glance

Materials

Focus Activity

Activity Objective

Activity

Metacognitive Processing

Bibliography

Academic preparation for college. (1983). New York: The College Board

An agenda for educational renewal: A report to the secretary of education, United States Department of Education. (1984). National Consortium for Educational Excellence. Nashville, TN: Vanderbilt University, Peabody College.

Ainsworth-Land, V., & Fletcher, N. (1979). *Making waves with creative problem solving.* Buffalo, NY: D.O.K.

Alexander, C., & Cowell, J. (1983). *Mapping insights.* Learning Insights.

Anderson, L.W., & Jones, B.F. (1981). Designing instructional strategies which facilitate learning for mastery. *Educational Psychologist, 16,* p. 121–138.

Anderson, R., & Pearson, P.D. (1985). A schema-thoretic view of basis processes in reading comprehension. In P.D. Pearson (Ed.), *Handbook of reading research.* New York: Longman.

Anderson, R. et al. (1985). *Becoming a nation of readers.* Commission on Reading of the National Academy of Education. Springfield, IL: Phillips Bros.

Anderson, T.H., & Armbruster, B.B. (1984). Content area textbooks. In R.C. Anderson, J. Osborn, R.J. Tierney (Eds.), *Learning to read in American schools: Basal readers and content texts.* Hillsdale, NJ: Erlbaum.

Armbruster, B.B., Echols, L.H., & Brown, A.L. (1983). *The role of metacognition in reading to learn: A developmental perspective* (p. 46-56). Urbana, IL: University of Illinois Center for the Study of Reading.

Bellanca, J. (1986). *Planning for thinking.* Palatine, IL: Skylight Publishing.

Bellanca, J. (1984). *Quality circles for educators.* Palatine, IL: Skylight Publishing.

Bellanca, J. (1984). *Skills for critical thinking.* Palatine, IL: Skylight Publishing.

Bellanca, J., & Fogarty, R. (1990). *Blueprints for thinking in the cooperative classroom.* Palatine, IL: Skylight Publishing.

Bellanca, J., & Fogarty, R. (1986). *Catch them thinking.* Palatine, IL: Skylight Publishing.

Berliner, D.C. (1984). The half-full glass: A review of research in teaching. In P.L. Hosford (Ed.), *Using what we know about teaching.* Alexandria, VA: Association for Supervision and Curriculum Development.

Beyer, B.K. (1983, November). Common sense about teaching thinking skills. *Educational Leadership,* p. 57-62.

Beyer, B.K. (1984, March). Improving thinking skills—defining the problem. *Phi Delta Kappan,* p. 486-490.

Biondi, A. (Ed.). (1972). *The creative process.* Buffalo, NY: D.O.K.

Black, H. and Black, S. (1981). *Figural analogies.* Pacific Grove, CA: Midwest Publications.

Bloom, B.S. (1981). *All our children learning. A primer for parents, teachers, and educators.* New York: McGraw-Hill.

Bloom, B.S. (Ed.). (1956). *Taxonomy of educational objectives: Cognitive domain.* New York: David McKay.

Brown, A.L. (1980). Metacognitive development and reading. In R.J. Spiro, B.C. Bruce, & W. F. Brewer (Eds.), *Theoretical issues in reading comprehension.* Hillsdale, NJ: Erlbaum.

Burns, M. (1976). *The book of think or how to solve a problem twice your size.* Boston, MA: Little, Brown and Company.

Campbell, T.C., Fuller, R.G., Thornton, M.C., Peter, J.L., Petterson, M.Q., Carpenter, E.T., & Narveson, R.D. (1980). A teacher's guide to the learning cycle. A Piagetian-based approach to college instruction. In R.G. Fuller, et al. (Eds.), *Piagetian programs in higher education* (p. 27-46). Lincoln, NE: ADAPT, University of Nebraska-Lincoln.

Carnine, D., & Silbert, J. (1979). *Direct instruction reading.* Columbus, OH: Merrill Publishing.

Carpenter, E.T. (1980). Piagetian interview of college students. R.G. Fuller, et al. (Eds.), *Piagetian programs in higher education* (pp. 15-21). Lincoln, NE: ADAPT, University of Nebraska-Lincoln.

Carpenter, T.P., Corbitt, M.K., Kepner, H., Linquist, M.M., & Reys, R.W. (1980, October). Students' affective responses to mathematics: National assessment results. *Educational Leadership,* p. 24-37, 52, 531-539.

Chase, L. (1975). *The other side of the report card.* Glenview, IL: Scott Foresman.

Clark, B. (1979). *Growing up gifted.* Columbus, OH: Merrill Publishing.

Clement, J. (1982). Algebra word problem solutions: Thought processes underlying a common misconception. *Journal for Research in Mathematics Education, 13,* p. 16-30.

Clement, J. (1982). Students' preconceptions in introductory mechanics. *American Journal of Physics, 50,* p. 66-71.

COGITARE. (1989 to Present). The quarterly newsletter for the ASCD's Network on Teaching Thinking. Palatine, IL: Skylight Publishing.

Convigtona, M.V., Crutchfield, R.S., Davies, L., & Olton, R.M. (1974). *The productive thinking program: A course in learning to think.* Columbus, OH: Merrill Publishing.

Costa, A.L. (Ed.). (1985). *Developing minds.* Alexandria, VA: Association for Supervision and Curriculum Development.

Costa, A.L. (1984, November). Mediating the metacognitive. *Educational Leadership,* p. 57-62.

Costa, A.L. (1981, October). Teaching for intelligent behavior. *Educational Leadership,* p.2 9-32.

Costa, A.L., & Lowery, L. (1989). *Techniques for teaching thinking.* Pacific Grove, CA: Midwest Publications.

Craik, F.I.M., & Lockhard, R.S. (1972). Levels of processing: Framework for memory research. *Journal of Verbal Learning and Verbal Behavior, II,* p. 671-684.

Creative cards: Attribute games and problems. (1966). New York: Webster Division of McGraw-Hill (ESS Science Series).

DeBoer, A.I. *The art of consulting.* Chicago, IL: Arcturus Books.

Duchastel, P.C. (1982). Textual display techniques. In D. Jonnasen (Ed.), *Principles for structuring, designing, and displaying text.* Englewood Cliffs, NJ: Educational Technology Publications.

Durkin, D. (1978-1979). What classroom observations reveal about reading comprehension instruction. *Reading Research Quarterly, 15,* p. 481-533.

Easterling, J., & Pasanen, J. (1979). *Confront, construct, complete.* Rochell Park, NJ: Hayden Publishing.

Eberle, B., & Stanish, B. (1980). *CPS for kids.* Buffalo, NY: D.O.K.

Eberle, B. (1982). *SCAMPER: Games for imagination development.* Buffalo, NY: D.O.K.

Eberle, B. (1982). *Visual thinking.* Buffalo, NY: D.O.K.

Edwards, B. (1979). *Drawing on the right side of the brain.* Los Angeles: J.P. Tarcher.

Eggen, Kauchak, & Harder. (1979). *Strategies for teachers.* New York: Prentice-Hall.

Elbow, P. (1973). *Writing without teachers.* New York: Oxford University Press.

Ellison, C. (1985, May 1). Science preparation of students, teachers is debated. *Education Week,* p. 26.

Ennis, R.H., & Norris, S.P. (1989). *Evaluating critical thinking.* Pacific Grove, CA: Midwest Publications.

Ferguson, M. (1980). *The aquarian conspiracy.* Los Angeles: J.P. Tarcher.

Feuerstein, R., & Jensen, M.R. (1980). Instructional enrichment: Theoretical bias, goals, and instruments. *The Education Form,* p. 401-423.

Fiestrizer, C.E. (1984). *The making of a teacher.* Washington, D.C.: National Center for Education Information.

Fiske, E. (1984, September 9). Concern over schools spurs extensive efforts at reform. *New York Times,* p. 1, 30.

50-state survey on critical thinking initiatives. (1985). Washington, D.C.: American Federation of Teachers.

Fogarty, R., & Bellanca, J. (1985). *Patterns for thinking—Patterns for transfer.* Palatine, IL: Skylight Publishing.

Fogarty, R., & Bellanca, J. (1986). *Teach them thinking.* Palatine, IL: Skylight Publishing.

Fogarty, R., & Haack, J. (1986). *The thinking log.* Palatine, IL: Skylight Publishing.

Fogarty, R., & Haack, J. (1988). *The thinking/writing connection.* Palatine, IL: Skylight Publishing.

Fogarty, R., & Opeka, K. (1988). *Start them thinking.* Palatine, IL: Skylight Publishing.

Gallagher, J. (1985). *Teaching the gifted child.* Boston: MA: Allyn & Bacon.

Gallelli, G. (1977). *Activity mindset guide.* Buffalo, NY: D.O.K.

Gardner, et al. (1983). *A nation at risk: The imperative for educational reform.* National Commission on Excellence in Education. Washington, DC: Department of Education.

Gifford, B.R. (1985, March 20). We must interrupt the cycle of minority-group failure. *Education Week, sec. IV,* p. 17-24.

Glatthorn, A. (1984). *Differentiated supervision.* Alexandria, VA: Association for Supervision and Curriculum Development.

Good, T.L. (1981, February). Teacher expectations and student perceptions. *Educational Leadership,* 415-422.

Good, T.L., & Brophy, J. E. (1984). *Looking in classrooms.* Cambridge, MA: Harper and Row.

Gordon, W.J.J. (1968). *Synectics: The development of creative capacity.* New York: Harper and Row.

Gordon, W.J.J., & Pose, T. *Activities in metaphor.* Cambridge, MA: Porpoise Books.

Gordon, W.J.J., & Pose, T. *Teaching is listening.* Cambridge, MA: Porpoise Books.

Guilford, J.P. (1975). *Way beyond the I.Q.* Buffalo, NY: Creative Education Foundation.

Hansen, J., & Pearson, P.D. (1983). An instructional study: Improving the inferential comprehension of good and poor fourth-grade readers. *Journal of Educational Psychology, 75,* p. 821-829.

Harnadek, A. (1977). *Basic thinking skills: Analogies-D.* Pacific Grove, CA: Midwest Publications.

Harnadek, A. (1977). *Basic thinking skills: Patterns*. Pacific Grove, CA: Midwest Publications.

Harnadek, A. (1980). *Critical thinking*. Pacific Grove, CA: Midwest Publications.

Herber, H.L. (1978). *Reading in the content areas: Text for teachers*. Englewood Cliffs, NJ: Prentice-Hall.

Hodgkinson, H.L. (1985). *All one system: Demography of schools, kindergarten through graduate school*. Washington, DC: Institute for Educational Leadership.

Howey, K., Matthes, W.A., & Zimpher, N.L. (1985, September). *Issues and problems in professional development*. Elmhurst, IL: Commissioned paper prepared for the North Central Regional Educational Laboratory.

Jenkins, J. (1974). Remember the old theory of memory? Well, forget it! *American Psychologist, 29,* p. 785-795.

Johnson, R. & Johnson, D. (1986). *Circles of learning: Cooperation in the classroom*. Alexandria, VA: Association for Supervision and Curriculum Development.

Johnson, R. & Johnson, D. (1987). *Learning together and alone: Cooperative, competitive, and individualistic learning*. New York: Prentice-Hall.

Jones, B.F., Amiran, M.R., & Katims, M. (1985). Teaching cognitive strategies and text structures within language arts programs. In S.F. Chipman & R. Glaser (Eds.), *Thinking and learning skills: Relating basic research to instructional practices, 1*. Hillsdale, NJ: Erlbaum.

Jones, B.F., & Spady, W.G. (1985). Enhanced mystery learning and quality of instruction. In D.V. Levine (Ed.), *Improving student achievement through mastery learning programs*. San Francisco, CA: Jossey-Bass.

Karplus, R. (1974). *Science curriculum improvement study, teachers handbook*. Berkeley, CA: University of California, Berkeley.

Larkin, J. (1983). Research on science education. In A.M. Lesgold & F. Reif (Eds.), *Education: Realizing the potential*. Washington, DC: Office of the Assisted Secretary for Educational Research and Improvement.

Larkin, J., McDermott, J., Simon, D.P., & Simon, H.A. (1980, June 20). Expert and novice performance in solving physics problems. *Science*, 1335-1342.

Maraviglia, C. (1978). *Creative problem-solving think book*. Buffalo, NY: D.O.K.

Maria, K., & McGinitie, W.H. (1982). Reading comprehension disabilities, knowledge structures, and non-accommodating text processing strategies. *Annuals of Dyslexia, 32,* p. 33-59.

Marcus, S.A., & McDonald, P. (1990). *Tools for the cooperative classroom*. Palatine, IL: Skylight Publishing.

Markle, S.M. (1975). They teach concepts, don't they? *Educational Researcher, 4,* p. 3-9.

Mayer, R.E. (1984). Aids to text comprehension. *Educational Psychologist, 19,* p. 30-42.

McCloskey, M., Carmazza, A., & Green, B. (1980, December 5). Curvillinear motion in the absence of external forces: Naive beliefs about the motion of objects. *Science,* p. 1139-1141.

The nation responds. (1984). National Commission on Excellence in Education. Washington, DC: Secretary of Education, U.S. Department of Education.

Nickerson, R.S. (1983). Computer programming as a vehicle for teaching thinking skills. *Journal of Philosophy for Children, 4,* p. 3-4.

Nickerson, R.S. (1982). *Understanding understanding* (BBN Report No. 5087).

Nickerson, R.S., Perkins, D.N., & Smith, E. E. (1984). *Teaching thinking* (BBN Report No. 5575).

Nickerson, R.S., Salter, W., Shepard & Herrnsteins, J. (1984). *The teaching of learning strategies* (BBN Report No. 5578).

Nisbett, R., & Ross, L. (1980). *Human inference: Strategies and shortcomings of social judgment.* Englewood Cliffs, NJ: Prentice-Hall.

Noller, R. (1977). *Scratching the surface of creative problem-solving: A bird's-eye view of CPS.* Buffalo, NY: D.O.K.

Noller, R., Parnes, S., & Bioni, A. (1976). *Creative action book.* New York: Charles Scribner and Sons.

Noller, R., Treffinger, D., & Houseman, E. (1979). *It's a gas to be gifted* or *CPS for the gifted and talented.* Buffalo, NY: D.O.K.

Osborn, A.F. (1963). *Applied imagination.* New York: Charles Scribner and Sons.

Palincsar, A.S., & Brown, A.L. (1985). Reciprocal activities to promote reading with your mind. In T.L. Harris & E. Cooper (Eds.), *Reading, thinking, and concept development: Strategies for the classroom.* New York: The College Board.

Parnes, S. (1975). *Aha! Insights into creative behavior.* Buffalo, NY: D.O.K.

Parnes, S. (1972). *Creativity: Unlocking human potential.* Buffalo, NY: D.O.K.

Pearson, P.D., & Leys, M. (1985). Teaching comprehension. In T.L. Harris & E. Cooper (Eds.), *Reading, thinking, and concept development: Strategies for the classroom.* New York: The College Board.

Perkins, D., & Swartz, R. (1989). *Teaching thinking: Issues and approaches.* Pacific Grove, CA: Midwest Publications.

Peters, T. & Austin, N. (1985). *Passion for excellence.* New York: Random House.

Peters, T. & Waterman, R., Jr. (1982). *In search of excellence*. New York: Warner Communication.

Polette, N. (1981). *Exploring books for gifted programs*. Metuchen, NJ: Scarecrow Press.

Raths, L. (1967). *Teaching for thinking*. Columbus, OH: Merrill Publishing.

Resnick, L.B. (1984). Cognitive science as educational research: Why we need it now. In *Improving education: Perspectives on educational research*. Pittsburgh, PA: University of Pittsburgh, Learning Research and Development Center.

Rico, G.L. (1983). *Writing the natural way*. Los Angeles, CA: J.P. Tarcher.

Rohwer, W.D. Jr. (1971). Prime time for education: Early childhood or adolescence? *Harvard Educational Review, 41,* p. 316-341.

Rosenshine, B. (1983). Teaching functions in instructional programs. *Elementary School Journal, 83,* 335-351.

Rosenshine, B., Harnischfeger, A., & Wallberg, H. (1985, March). *Classroom programs for school improvement*. Elmhurst, IL: An Advisory paper for the North Central Regional Educational Laboratory.

Rowe, M.B. (1969). Science, silence and sanctions. *Science & Children, 6,* p. 11-13.

Rumelhart, D.E. (1980). Schemata: The building blocks of cognition. In R.J. Spiro, B.C. Bruce & W.F. Brewer (Eds.), *Theoretical issues in reading comprehension*. Hillsdale, NJ: Erlbaum.

Scardamalia, M., Bereiter, C., & Fillion B. (1979). *The little red writing book: A source book of consequential writing activities*. Toronto, Ontario: Pedagogy of Writing Project, O.I.S.E.

Schallert, D.L. (1980). The role of illustrations in reading comprehension. In R.J. Spiro, B.C. Bruce & W. F. Brewer (Eds.), *Theoretical issues in reading comprehension*. Hillsdale, NJ: Erlbaum.

Schoenfeld, A.H. (1980). Teaching problem-solving skills. *American Mathematical Monthly, 87*(10), p. 794-805.

Shuell, T.J. (1984, October). *The concept of learning in modern-day cognitive psychology*. Ellenville, New York: Paper presented at the annual meeting of the Northeastern Educational Research Association.

Shulman, L.S. (1984). Understanding pedagogy: Research for the improvement of teaching and teacher education. In *Improving education: Perspectives on educational research*. Pittsburgh, PA: University of Pittsburgh, Learning Research and Development Center.

Sirkin, J.R. (1985, May 8). All-black education agenda advocated: Press for excellence seen at odds with equity goal. *Education Week, sec. IV,* p. 1, 27.

Snyder, D.P. (1985). *The strategic context of education in America* (Future-Research Tech. Rep.). Washington, DC: National Education Association, Professional and Organization Development/Office of Planning.

Spiro, R. (1980). Constructive processes in prose comprehension and recall. In R.J. Spiro, B.C. Bruce, & W.F. Brewer (Eds.), *Theoretical issues in reading comprehension*. Hillsdale, NJ: Erlbaum.

Sternberg, R.J. (1981, October). Intelligence as thinking and learning skills. *Educational Leadership,* p. 18-21.

Task Force on Education for Economic Growth. (1983). *Action for excellence: A comprehensive plan to improve our nation's schools*. Washington, DC: Education Commission of the United States.

Teacher preparation: The anatomy of a college degree. (1985). Atlanta, GA: The Southern Regional Education Board.

Tolkien, J.R.R. (1937). *The hobbit.* New York: Ballantine Books.

Torrance, E.P. (1979). *The search for satori and creativity.* Buffalo, NY: Creative Education Foundation and Great Neck, NY: Creative Synergetics Associates.

Trowbridge, D.E., & McDermott, L.C. (1980). Investigation of student understanding of the concept of velocity in one dimension. *American Journal of Physics, 48*(12), p. 1010-1028.

Tversky, A., & Kahneman, D. (1974, September 27). Judgment under uncertainty: Heuristics and biases. *Science,* p. 1124-1131.

Underwood, V.L. (1982). *Self-management skills for college students: A program in how to learn.* Unpublished doctoral dissertation, University of Texas.

von Oech, R. (1983). *A whack on the side of the head.* New York: Warner Books.

Who's keeping score? (1980). National Institute of Education. Washington, DC: McLeod Corporation.

Notes

Notes

Notes

Notes

Notes

Notes

Notes

Additional resources to increase your teaching expertise...

There are

one-story intellects,

two-story intellects, and three-story

intellects with skylights. All fact collectors who have

no aim beyond their facts are one-story men. Two-story men compare,

reason, generalize, using the labor of fact collectors as their own.

Three-story men idealize, imagine, predict—

lumination comes

ve the skylight.

ver *Wendell*

Holmes

DATE DUE

IGHT

SHING, INC.